Lookin' Good,
beetle bailey

Lookin' Good, beetle bailey
by Mort Walker

tempo
books

GROSSET & DUNLAP
A FILMWAYS COMPANY
Publishers • New York

ZERO, YOU'RE STANDING IN MY LIGHT

10-29

NOW YOU'RE STANDING IN MY SHADE

© King Features Syndicate, Inc., 1978. World rights reserved.

I'M BEGINNING TO GET THE DRIFT

MORT WALKER

I THINK YOU HAVE THE WRONG NUMBER. WHO WERE YOU TRYING TO CALL?

THE ENLISTED MEN'S BENEVOLENT SOCIETY.

BOY, HAVE **YOU** GOT THE WRONG NUMBER!

BEETLE'S IN THE HOSPITAL?!

YEAH, WE'D BETTER VISIT HIM WHILE THERE'S STILL TIME

11-29

SOUNDS SERIOUS! WHAT'S HIS PROBLEM?

TERMINAL INSUBORDINATION

FAT JERK

MORT WALKER

SIR, DID YOU MAKE THIS STATEMENT THAT GRIPING WAS HEALTHY?

YES

11-30

A SOLDIER WHO GRIPES IS ALIVE AND INTERESTED. IT'S **APATHY** I DON'T LIKE

YOU'RE GOING TO LIKE THIS, THEN, SIR

BETTER FOOD

SHORTER HOURS

MORT WALKER

12-1

THE GENERAL WANTS TO SEE YOU

DOES HE WANT TO GIVE DICTATION?

12-23

NO, HE'S BEEN REVIEWING TROOPS ALL MORNING AND HAS "KHAKI EYES"

JUST STAND THERE A MINUTE

1-20

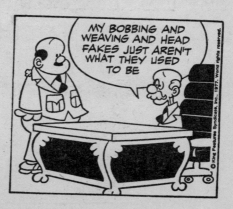

BEETLE? IS THAT YOU?

YES, SIR!

SLAM!!

2-7

DO YOU KNOW SARGE HAS BEEN LOOKING EVERYWHERE FOR YOU?!

RELAX. HE FOUND ME

MORT WALKER

Dear Diary!
there is a woman on the post that we will have to do something about.

The men cannot deal with her presence in a rational manner. the mere sight of her makes them tremble.

Her name is Mrs Bulley!

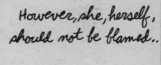

However, she, herself, should not be blamed..

MORT WALKER

3-3